OUR DOG WAS
OUR TEACHER

*An interactive book designed
to aid grieving and healing.
A Memory Keepsake of Your Dog*

By Joyce Johnson

Illustrated by
Vickie Leigh Krudwig

To Sally & Ed,
Animal lovers
through & through,
you've had many
"teachers" in
your family!
Love,
Joyce

ZECHARIAH
PUBLISHING

Arvada, Colorado

OUR DOG WAS OUR TEACHER
An interactive book designed to aid grieving and healing.
A Memory Keepsake of Your Dog

Library of Congress Control Number: 2007935527

ISBN 978-0-9796770-0-7

1. Non-fiction, 2. Juvenile literature, 3. Children and death, 4. Bereavement,
5. Pets - illness - death - psychological aspects, 6. Human - Animal Bonding, 7. Family healing.

First Printing: September 2007
Printed in the United States

Produced and distributed by

ZECHARIAH
PUBLISHING

P. O. Box 740182
Arvada, CO 80006
(303) 829-4565
j2j445@msn.com

This book is dedicated to all families
who are still missing their beloved dog.

FOREWORD

Communication with children over sad losses helps the child express their feelings, which is the first step in the healing process. This sense of loss lingers over varying periods of time and parents should be aware of signs where the child might be missing their pet. A special time or walk with the child, addressing the sadness, can help. Advice giving is usually not necessary; however, listening and empathy is most productive. Affirmation of the child's feelings is part of this process. All members of the family grieve over the loss of a pet, and a family meeting may be helpful as well.

Many parents are lost in how they should communicate with their children over such a loss, as they are grieving themselves. This is why Joyce Johnson's sensitive, structured, and interactive book helps both children and their parents turn sad memories into positive remembrances.

Larry Seid, Ph.D
Educator and Counselor

INTRODUCTION

Our dog, Ben, was a special dog. I knew he was special the very first time I saw him. I saw the excitement and happiness in his whole being when he first met us. I took into consideration the fact that he had barked and growled at several prospective families prior to our arrival. His excitement and happiness at seeing us was both contagious, and also a confirmation that we were to be HIS family. I accepted this fact, but I still wondered why. Why did he choose us? As you read, you will see that He was in charge.

It really wasn't until after Ben died and after much grieving that I came to know the reason. He came to be our teacher! I also learned that an "attitude of gratitude" is one of the best remedies for depression. Once you and your family begin to be aware of, and be grateful for, all the little things you "learned" from your dog, then the healing will begin.

This book is designed for active participation. At first you may just want to read it through and think about it. After while, I encourage all family members to be involved in creating this special keepsake for your dog. Write, draw, add photos, create poetry and music. Do whatever feels right. Your dog was with you for a reason and as you remember and explore your time together with him, you too, will find out WHY, and be grateful.

Joyce Johnson

When our dog, Ben, died, I was very, very sad………..and I cried. Our whole family cried. If your special dog is sick, it's okay to be sad. If your special dog was sick and died or had an accident and died, it's okay for you to cry and be sad.

After his death I began to think about all the happy memories we had with Ben.

This is one of my favorite pictures of Ben. It's hard to tell who is smiling the most- Paula, Eric, Brian or Ben.

LESSON
It's Okay to be sad.

MEET MY DOG!

I am sure you have many happy memories of your dog. Writing some special memories about your dog will help to heal some of your sadness.

My dog's name: _____

His/her breed: _____

Date of Birth or Adoption: _____

Paste or draw a picture of your dog in the box. What color fur did your dog have? What color were his/her eyes?

It all started when my son Brian told me he wanted a dog. Brian would wish upon a star for a dog.

Brian would throw a penny in a fountain and make a wish for a dog.

When Brian said his prayers every night, we would pray for a special dog.

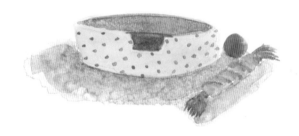

LESSON
Don't give up if you have a special dream.

HOW I GOT MY DOG

Do you remember how your family decided to get a dog? Write about your experience here:

_____

_____

_____

_____

_____

_____

_____

Who, in your family, wanted a dog? _____

_____

_____

_____

_____

_____

_____

Why did you want a dog? _____

_____

_____

_____

_____

_____

Anytime YOU think of a lesson that your dog taught you, you can write it at the bottom of your page.

_____

_____

_____

_____

_____

_____

_____

Finally we decided it was time to adopt a dog. First, Brian got books from the library about dogs. Since Brian's brother Eric had allergies, we had to find a dog that would not shed. We found out that dogs that have some poodle hair will not shed.

Then we looked in the newspaper under "Dogs For Sale". Soon Brian found an ad for a cocker spaniel/poodle mix dog. The day I called, the lady said there were many people already coming to see her dog that night and we could call the next morning to see if she still had him. She said she was going to be very particular about the family who got him.

Brian said a special prayer that night.

DOGS FOR SALE

Adorable puppies and kittens for sale. Free vet exam and health guarantee. Shots and worming up-to-date.

Cockapoo & Terrier pups. Health guar. Ready now.

COCKER PUPPIES: AKC Ready 3:2:2 Litters. Del. Avail.

LESSON
Always do your homework; and always say your prayers.

FINDING MY DOG

How did you find your dog? _____ _____

_____

_____

_____

_____

Did you look in the newspaper? _____

_____

_____

_____

_____

Did you look at a pet store or animal shelter? _____

_____

_____

_____

_____

_____

**Paste or draw a
picture of your dog
on the day you got it.**

The next morning I called the lady. She said Ben barked and growled at all the people who came to see him, so she still had him. She would not give him to someone he didn't like. She said we could come and see him, but she was worried because it was unusual for Ben to growl and bark. If he did the same thing when we came, she just couldn't let him go with us. She wanted him to be happy with his new family.

LESSON
Trust

NAMING MY DOG

Our dog already had a name. Did your dog have a name, or did you pick a name?

_____
_____
_____
_____
_____
_____
_____

How did you decide on your dog's name? _____
_____
_____
_____
_____
_____

Brian and Eric had to go to school that morning, so my daughter Paula and I drove to the lady's house. Paula told me that she was praying all the way there.

We rang the doorbell and heard a little "woof-woof" on the other side of the door.

When the lady opened the door, Ben jumped up on us and kissed us all over, wagged his tail and danced all around us. It was like he had been waiting just for us and he was so happy to see us. The lady was very surprised. She said, "Well, it looks like Ben picked you!"

Ben could hardly wait to go jump into our car and go home with us.

"The reason a dog has so many friends is that he wags his tail instead of his tongue."
Author Unknown

LESSON
God answers our prayers.

HOW I MET MY DOG

Do you remember when you first saw your dog? _____

_____

_____

_____

_____

_____

_____

What did you do? _____

_____

_____

_____

_____

_____

_____

How did you feel? _____

_____

_____

_____

_____

_____

What did your dog do? _____

_____

_____

_____

_____

We were the lucky family that Ben picked. We liked him the minute we saw him and felt those sloppy wet kisses. He was black, soft and fuzzy with a big tail that didn't stop wagging. He had a happy dance and big brown eyes.

When we got home, Ben went all over our house smelling everything and wagging his tail. We told him there were two big brothers and a Dad in our family who were going to be so happy to see him. We let Ben smell some of their clothes while we talked to him.

LESSON
Animals show love by always listening to us.
We can show love by listening too.

TALKING WITH MY DOG

Did you talk with your dog? _____

_____

_____

_____

_____

_____

_____

_____

What things did you say? _____

_____

_____

_____

_____

_____

_____

_____

_____

How did you know your dog was listening? _____

_____

_____

_____

_____

_____

_____

_____

_____

Ben was happy to see Brian and Eric and they got lots of dances and happy doggie kisses too.

Ben was about two years old when we got him. He was already house broken and didn't even jump on the furniture. We had to teach him that it was okay to sleep on Brian's bed that night.

When Dad got home from work, he said, "He looks like a nice dog, but the newness will soon wear off, and then no one will pay any attention to him". We answered, "No sir, we love this dog."

*"We long for an affection
altogether ignorant of our faults.
Heaven has accorded this
to us in the uncritical
canine attachment.*
George Eliot

LESSON
Dogs know when you love them and want them.

BECOMING A FAMILY MEMBER

How old was your dog when he came to your house? _____
_____
_____
_____
_____
_____

Did you help train your dog? _____
_____
_____
_____
_____
_____

What kinds of commands did your dog learn? _____
_____
_____
_____
_____
_____
_____

Where did your dog sleep?
_____
_____
_____
_____
_____
_____
_____
_____

Ben wanted to learn everything we could teach him.

He learned, "sit" and "stay".

He learned, "down" and "jump".

He learned, "shake hands" and "high five".

He learned, "guess which hand" and "go to your place".

He learned, "hide and seek". He was better at finding than hiding. Ben loved dog treats. We called them cookies because his box of treats was in the same cupboard with our cookies.

LESSON
Learning new things can be fun.

MY SMART DOG

What things did you teach your dog? _____

_____

_____

_____

_____

_____

_____

Did your dog like to play games? What kind of games? _____

_____

_____

_____

_____

What were your dog's favorite toys?

_____

_____

_____

_____

_____

_____

_____

_____

_____

"Animals are such
agreeable friends--
they ask no questions,
they pass no criticisms."
George Eliot

One night when Brian, Eric and Paula were getting ready for bed, I called them into our kitchen for their bedtime snack. I said, "Here are your cookies, hurry with your snack, because it is late and we have to be up early tomorrow." I handed each a cookie. In a little while, Paula come into the kitchen and said, "Where is my cookie?" Just then we all noticed Ben chomping a cookie and wagging his tail.

LESSON

Everyone should have a bedtime snack.

YUMMIES

Did your dog like treats? _____

_____

_____

_____

What kind did he like best? _____

_____

_____

_____

**"The dog was created especially for children.
He is a god of frolic."**
Henry Ward Beecher

Paste your dog's picture in the box or draw a picture of him/her eating her favorite treat.

In the mornings Ben thought it was great fun to grab Brian and Eric's socks and run away so they would have to chase him all around the house. When they finally got the socks back and walked out the door, Ben would watch through the window and cry little whimper sounds as they walked away to school.

He was so happy to see them when they got home, and he couldn't wait to hear them tell him all about their day at school. Then Ben was ready to play anything they wanted.

LESSON
Dogs are always happy to see you.
They listen to you, and they like you just the way you are!

WELCOME HOME!

Was your dog happy to see you when you came home?

_____

_____

_____

_____

_____

_____

_____

_____

_____

_____

What did your dog do to welcome you?

_____

_____

_____

_____

_____

_____

_____

_____

Ben liked playing whatever game the kids played. He loved playing soccer, playing catch, and going for walks.

Paula played school with Ben. She read stories to him, played dress-up games, and even ate lunch with Ben. (Lunchtime was his favorite.)

In the fall, he jumped into piles of leaves and in the winter he liked riding the sled down hill.

We have silly pictures of him wearing sunglasses and hats and different shirts.

LESSON
Be thankful for all the silly and happy days with your dog.

FUN AND GAMES

Do you have silly pictures of your dog? Paste them in the boxes below!

What games did your dog like best? _____
_____
_____
_____
_____
_____
_____
_____
_____

One day, a kitten we named KiKi came to live with us. Ben was very happy to have a new friend. He liked all animals. Ben especially liked being a big brother to KiKi, and they also became best friends. They even took naps together.

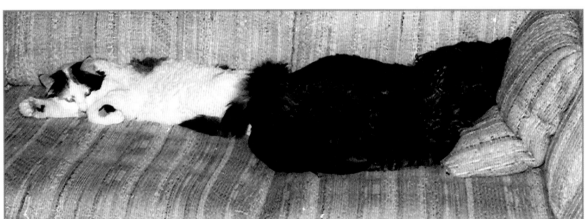

LESSON
New friends are interesting, especially if they are different.

MY FAMILY'S OTHER PETS

Did your family have other pets? _____

What were their names _____

_____

_____

_____

_____

_____

How did your dog treat them? _____

_____

_____

_____

_____

_____

Draw or paste a picture of your other pets in the box.

I think Ben's favorite thing to do was to go for a walk. We soon learned that we had to spell out "w-a-l-k" because as soon as he heard us say the word "walk", he would jump up and down, do his happy dance, and run into the pantry and get his leash and bring it to us. He would be so excited that he couldn't stop dancing and jumping until we walked out the door and began the walk to the park.

Spelling worked for a little while, but he soon figured out what we were spelling and off he went dancing and jumping and getting his leash. Then we had to spell it backwards "k-l-a-w".

LESSON
Dogs are very smart.

GOING PLACES WITH MY DOG

Did your dog like to go for walks? Where did you go? _____

_____

_____

_____

_____

_____

Did your dog like to ride in the car? _____

_____

_____

_____

_____

_____

What was your dog's favorite thing to do? _____

_____

_____

_____

_____

"My little dog --
a heartbeat at my feet."
Edith Wharton

Ben was a pretty healthy dog and just needed to go to the vet for the usual check-ups and shots. But one day he became very ill. He had to have an operation and stay overnight at the animal hospital.

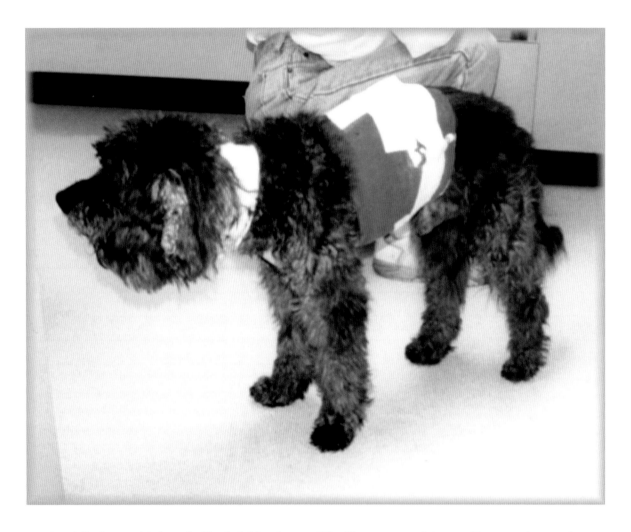

Luckily for us, this hospital had visiting hours. We all went to see him, and because he was happy to be with us for a little while, it helped him get better faster.

LESSON
Be thankful to our animal doctors who help our pets feel better.

CARING FOR MY DOG

Did you go with you dog to the vet? What was the veterinarian's name? _____

_____

_____

_____

_____

Did your dog ever get sick? _____

_____

_____

_____

_____

What happened? _____

_____

_____

_____

_____

"One reason a dog can be such a comfort when you're feeling blue is that he doesn't try to find out why."
Author Unknown

After many years, our Ben was getting very old. He couldn't hear or see very well. He still liked going for walks, even though it was hard for him to go up and down the stairs. Sometimes I had to carry him up the steps.

LESSON
Animals get old faster than people.
We still love and care for them when they are old.

HELPING MY SICK DOG

If your dog was sick, who helped take care of him?

_____

_____

_____

_____

_____

_____

_____

_____

_____

_____

What did the veterinarian do to help your dog? _____

_____

_____

_____

_____

_____

_____

_____

_____

_____

_____

_____

What kind of things did you do to comfort your dog? _____

_____

_____

_____

_____

_____

_____

_____

_____

_____

_____

One day I came home from work, and Ben didn't greet me at the door. He was still laying where I had put him at lunchtime. He wagged his tail a little when he saw me, so I picked him up and took him outside to go potty. That's when I found out he was too weak to stand up.

Early the next morning we all gathered around Ben at Dr. Carpenter's office. Ben was very weak and tired looking. Dr. Carpenter told us to talk with him. He said Ben could still hear us, and it would help him to say good-bye to us. We told him how much we loved him. We thanked him for picking us to be his family. We thanked him for all the things he taught us. We thanked him for being our teacher. We said good-bye. We were very sad and we cried.

LESSON
Grown ups have to make hard choices.

WHEN MY DOG DIED

All dogs get old and tired and sometimes very sick before they die. Dogs can also have accidents and die.

When did your pet die? _____
_____
_____
_____
_____
_____

Was your dog old? _____
_____

Was your dog sick? _____
_____

Did your dog have an accident? _____
_____

Our family still misses Ben very much. Dad even said he was wrong; the "newness" never did wear off. Even though we don't have that warm fuzzy dog to play with now, we still have all these wonderful memories of him. In fact, it helps us to talk about him when we get sad from thinking about Ben.

We thought we were teaching him lots of things, but Ben taught us the most important things:

He taught us about saying good-bye to someone we love.

He taught us that our special memories will live forever.

Ben taught us that love never dies.

LESSON
Our love never dies.

SAYING GOODBYE

Were you able to say good-bye to your dog before he died? You can still talk to your dog. Think about your dog, and tell your dog all the things you had fun doing with him.

_____
_____
_____
_____
_____
_____
_____
_____
_____
_____
_____
_____
_____
_____
_____
_____
_____
_____
_____
_____
_____
_____
_____

"You think dogs will not be in heaven?
I tell you, they will be there long before any of us."
Robert Louis Stevenson

OTHER THINGS I WOULD LIKE TO TELL

_____

(Your dog's name)

Think about your dog, and tell him about how glad you are that he came to live with you. I'm sure your dog taught you many things. Thank him for all the things you learned. Tell your dog that you will miss him, and that you will never, ever, forget him.

Dear _____,

_____

_____

_____

_____

_____

_____

_____

_____

Love,

_____

PICTURES AND MEMORIES OF MY DOG

MY SPECIAL DOG

Here is space for you to tell more about your dog. You may put more pictures, draw, and write YOUR story about your special dog. It well help heal some of your hurt and you will feel a little better every day.

SPECIAL KEEPSAKES FROM MY DOG

LESSONS FROM MY DOG

Write about some of the lessons your dog taught you.

1. _____

2. _____

3. _____

4. _____

5. _____

6. _____

7. _____

8. _____

9. _____

10. _____

God created your dog for a special purpose.
God created you for a special reason too.
You are here so you can teach someone.
What will you teach?

ABOUT THE AUTHOR

Joyce Johnson was born in Wisconsin, into a large family of eight siblings, and a dog named Foxie. She moved to Colorado in 1964, and has lived in Arvada, Colorado for over 35 years.

Joyce is married and has three grown children and nine grandchildren. Ben was the first family pet; followed by Kiki (their cat teacher), and Kaeksa, a dog who lives with Joyce and her husband, Roger today.

Her training and volunteer work with Hospice and Stephen's Ministry, and her love of children and animals helped inspire Joyce to write this book. Joyce's second book, *Our Cat Was Our Teacher* will be released in the near future.

*15% of sales are being donated to Hospice of Peace.

To place an order for additional books,
please write, call or email:

Zechariah Publishing

P. O. Box 740182
Arvada, CO 80006
(303) 829-4565

j2j445@msn.com

COMING SOON:
Our Cat Was Our Teacher